A TRUE BOOK™

Quicksand

Gambino

S T E V E N   O T F I N O S K I

Children's Press®
An Imprint of Scholastic Inc.

Content Consultant
William Barnart, PhD
Assistant Professor
Department of Earth and Environmental Sciences
University of Iowa
Iowa City, Iowa

Library of Congress Cataloging-in-Publication Data
Otfinoski, Steven, author.
Quicksand / by Steven Otfinoski.
pages cm. — (A true book)
Includes bibliographical references and index.
ISBN 978-0-531-22295-9 (library binding) — ISBN 978-0-531-22511-0 (pbk.)
1. Quicksand—Juvenile literature. I. Title. II. Series: True book.
QE471.2.O84 2016
552.5—dc23   2015020987

© 2016 Scholastic Inc.
All rights reserved. Published in 2016 by Children's Press, an imprint of Scholastic Inc.
Printed in the U.S.A. 08
SCHOLASTIC, CHILDREN'S PRESS, A TRUE BOOK™, and associated logos are trademarks and/or registered trademarks of Scholastic Inc.
2 3 4 5 6 7 8 9 10 R 25 24 23 22 21 20 19 18 17 16

Front cover: A baby zebra is helped by a rhino to escape from a mud pit
Back cover: A sign warns of quicksand at an excavation site

Find the Truth!

Everything you are about to read is true *except* for one of the sentences on this page.

Which one is **TRUE**?

T or F   Quicksand can be any kind of soil that is changed by a steady flow of water.

T or F   Most quicksand sucks people and animals down quickly, with little hope of escape.

Find the answers in this book.

3

Contents

THE **BIG** TRUTH!

Dry Quicksand

Buildings after the 1906 San Francisco earthquake

5 Quicksand's Deadly Cousin

How is quick clay different from quicksand?..... **37**

Quick clay liquefies almost instantly.

5

The forests of the northwestern United States might be the last place you would expect to find quicksand.

CHAPTER 1

Stuck

It was a normal Saturday early in the spring of 2011 in Spokane, Washington. Friends Katie and Carl Hiatt and Andrew and Caleb Hummel met up to play. The children decided to go exploring in the forest near their houses. They didn't travel far into the woods before they came across a big mud pit. It looked like the perfect place to play.

Most quicksand pools are only a few feet deep.

A Near Tragedy

The mud was not as safe as it seemed. Andrew's foot soon became stuck in it. He saw that Katie and Carl were both starting to sink, too. The three friends struggled to pull themselves out. Carl managed to escape, but Katie and Andrew were trapped. In fact, their efforts only made them sink deeper. The mud was very cold. The friends were becoming scared. Caleb ran for help.

Mud pits and similar places are a common sight across much of the United States' wooded areas.

It is often best to call firefighters or other rescue workers for help in emergencies, such as if someone sinks into quicksand.

Caleb told the first adult he found about the emergency. The man called 911. By the time firefighters arrived, the mud had reached Katie's chest. "She was shivering real bad," said firefighter John Merrick. "I climbed in the mud with her to start digging her out." It took about 30 minutes to pull both children to safety. The children were cold but uninjured.

How could mud have been so dangerous? Underneath this mud was quicksand.

LE PETIT JOURNAL

ILLUSTRÉ

HEBDOMADAIRE - 36ᵉ Année
61, rue Lafayette, Paris

17 Mai 1925. - N 1795
PRIX : 30 CENTIMES

In 1925, the quicksand at Mont Saint-Michel claimed the life of a local woman.

UN DRAMATIQUE ENLISEMENT

CHAPTER 2

Just Add Water

What do you imagine when you think of quicksand? Do incidents such as the mud pit in Washington come to mind? Perhaps you've seen a movie with an adventurous young explorer walking down a twisting jungle path. He suddenly feels the ground giving way under his feet. The wet sand sucks him down until he is up to his waist in it, then deeper. Only his head sticks out of the pool. That too is then swallowed up by the thick muck.

Mont Saint-Michel in France is famous for the dangerous quicksand that surrounds it.

Low tide reveals an area of dry land and quicksand between mainland France and the island Mont Saint-Michel.

A Movie Myth

Scenes like that make an exciting story, but it's more fiction than fact. Quicksand doesn't suck people completely under. In truth, people float in it. Most don't sink past their waist. Struggling can make people sink faster. Even then, most quicksand pools are only a few feet deep. If a person stays calm, he or she can usually escape safely. Quicksand can be dangerous. But when you know the facts, you can survive it.

What Is Quicksand?

Quicksand doesn't actually work quickly. Also, it is not always sand. In fact, any soil can become quicksand. The main ingredient needed to turn sand, dirt, or gravel into quicksand is water. Ordinary soil is made up of tiny grains bound tightly together to form solid ground. When it mixes with water in just the right way, the ground turns mushy and can no longer support weight.

Signs warn visitors about quicksand in Morecambe Bay in England.

SOUTH LAKELAND DISTRICT COUNCIL

DANGEROUS FOR SWIMMING
BEWARE INCOMING TIDES
QUICKSANDS AND DEEP GULLIES

IN EMERGENCY PHONE 999 AND ASK FOR COASTGUARD

13

Quicksand can occur wherever there is water. Damp jungles, marshes, lakes, beaches, and land along streams are all places where you might find quicksand. Quicksand usually forms in connection with underground streams or springs in these areas. There, water constantly flows in from underneath to **saturate** the ground. This agitates, or moves, the grains of soil, pushing them apart and allowing more water to flow in. As a result, the ground transforms into quicksand.

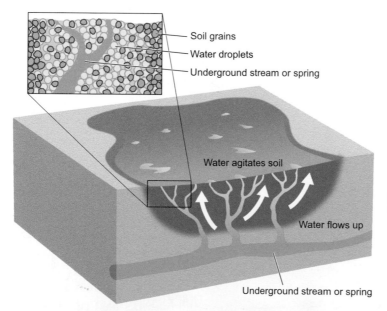

Soil grains
Water droplets
Underground stream or spring

Water agitates soil

Water flows up

Underground stream or spring

Quicksand is rarely found in deserts, where there is little or no water.

Depending on the mixture of sand and water, your feet might sink just enough to leave a clear footprint, or you might sink much deeper.

At the Beach

Beaches are perfect places for quicksand because of the combination of sand and water. The driest part of the beach is firm because the sand grains are packed tightly together and mostly dry. But closer to the water, the sand becomes less firm. This is because of the flow of seawater over and under the sand. In some places, enough water may constantly flow up from underneath. Then beach sand turns to quicksand.

The 1906 San Francisco earthquake and fires left half of the city's population homeless.

Earthquakes

Most quicksand is created slowly and in the same way it is made on beaches. But there is another way quicksand can be made, and it can happen with great suddenness. Earthquakes shake and break Earth's surface. In doing so, they can cause water to move around in the soil and force soil grains apart. This sudden saturation can **liquefy** the ground and create quicksand.

This kind of quicksand can be far more dangerous. It threatens not only buildings, but also people and animals. As the earth softens, buildings can collapse or sink. When an earthquake struck the city of Niigata, Japan, in 1964, the earth turned to quicksand. Apartment buildings fell over onto their sides. People had to climb out of the windows to exit the buildings safely. Fortunately, such quicksand is rarely that severe.

Residents climb out their windows and walk along the wall of their fallen apartment building in Niigata, Japan, after the earthquake in 1964.

There has been a royally chosen guide in England since the 16th century to help people cross Morecambe Bay safely.

CHAPTER 3

A World of Shifting Sands

Quicksand can be found around the world. However, there are certain areas that are particularly famous—or infamous—for quicksand. Travelers have learned over time to avoid such places at all costs. One example is Morecambe Bay. This vast region of **mudflats** and sand lies along the coast of northwestern England. It covers 120 square miles (311 square kilometers). The area is a place of great natural beauty and great danger.

Dangerous Waters

Quicksand on the mudflats of Morecambe Bay has long been known to trap fishers and swimmers. When the tide sweeps in, the visitors are unable to move, and they drown. In the early 1800s, horse-drawn coaches crossing the area would sink or be overturned in the quicksand. It was so dangerous that officials stopped the coach service in 1857.

An abandoned car is partially buried in the sand at Morecambe Bay.

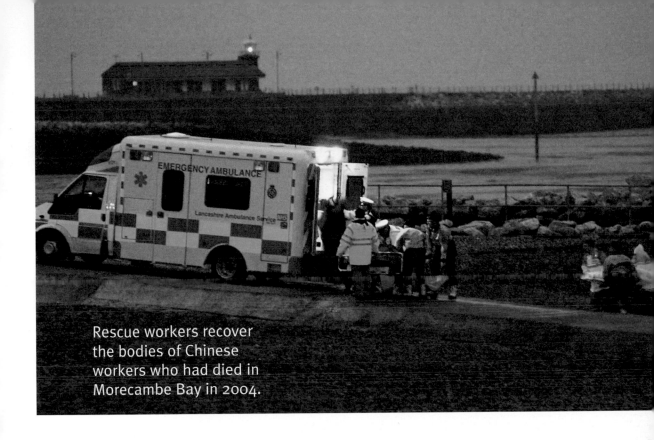

Rescue workers recover the bodies of Chinese workers who had died in Morecambe Bay in 2004.

In 2004, 24 Chinese immigrant workers were gathering shellfish along the beaches of the bay at night. The tide rolled in suddenly. The workers became stuck in the sinking sand and were unable to reach dry land. One called frantically for help on his cell phone. "Sinking water," he said. "Many, many sinking water." Only one person survived, rescued by a helicopter.

Salt can make quicksand more unstable and dangerous.

A thin crust of salt is often found covering areas with quicksand in the Rub' al-Khali Desert.

Mother of Poison

Deserts have little water and rarely have quicksand. But there are exceptions. The Rub' al-Khali in Saudi Arabia and Oman is the largest sand desert in the world. It spans 250,000 square miles (647,497 sq km). One corner is covered with salt marshes. This area is called Umm al Samim, or "Mother of Poison." Under a thin top crust hides dangerous quicksand. Over the years, goat herds and whole **caravans** of people have disappeared there.

Graveyard for Tanks

Another desert famous for quicksand is the Qattara Depression in northwestern Egypt. This region contains the second-lowest point in Africa. It is 436 feet (133 meters) below sea level. Like the Rub' al-Khali, Qattara's salt marshes are dotted with quicksand. During the 1942 Battle of El Alamein in World War II (1939–1945), some tanks and other military vehicles became permanently trapped in it.

Troops from around the world lost tanks to the quicksand around the El Alamein battle zone.

Quicksand in the United States

Quicksand is found across the United States. It is particularly common in Georgia, Florida, and North Carolina. In the Southwest, salt **erodes** from sandstone canyons and enters the soil. This makes the soil less stable, increasing the risk of quicksand. In July 2014, friends of a 78-year-old woman reported her missing in Utah. Police found her trapped in quicksand in Arches National Park where she worked. She had been there for 14 hours. It took four people to help her out.

Quicksand is a fairly common danger in parts of Utah, including Arches National Park.

Dinosaur Bones

Most people see quicksand as a danger, as they should. However, it can also have great value. In 2001, researchers found a massive collection of dinosaur **fossils** in Utah's sandstone. Scientists believe the animals died in quicksand. When one dinosaur became trapped, it attracted hungry **predators**, which then also became trapped and eventually died. Buried in sand and protected from wind and rain, the animals were preserved as fossils over millions of years.

Stuck in the Muck

People rarely die in quicksand, but it does pose dangers if someone becomes trapped in it. These dangers include being left exposed to the hot sun or intense cold, as well as rain or snow. Intense cold may cause **hypothermia**. Someone who is trapped for an extended period might starve or die of thirst. If the quicksand is along the shore, a trapped person could drown when the tide comes in.

Rescue workers in quicksand-prone areas regularly practice how to rescue a person from quicksand.

You can escape quicksand if you remain calm and have patience.

Lifting one leg directly out of quicksand can require the same force it takes to lift a car.

Escape

Even though quicksand is dangerous, it doesn't mean you should never go exploring in the great outdoors. There are steps you can take to avoid quicksand. If you do stumble into it, there's no need to panic. You can escape safely if you remain calm and know what to do.

Know Where You Are

The best way to escape quicksand is to avoid it. Know the area where you are. If there are quicksand pools, learn their locations and stay away from them. A pool might be new or unexpected. If the ground looks wet, test it with a walking stick. If the stick sinks, the ground may be quicksand. Also, you can't always see quicksand. Leaves or other **debris** may cover its surface. Tread carefully wherever there's a risk of quicksand.

A woman in Utah tests the depth of a pool for possible quicksand.

Have a Hiking Buddy

Always hike with a friend, especially in areas you don't know. If you step into quicksand, your buddy can call 911 or go get help. Quicksand is incredibly heavy, and if you fall in, your weight will push water out of the sand, making it even more solid around you. It may not be possible for your friend to pull you out, and it can be dangerous to try. You could get hurt being pulled, and you also risk pulling your friend in with you.

Timeline of Major Quicksand Moments

1964
An earthquake in Niigata, Japan, transforms the ground to quicksand. Several buildings collapse.

2004
Twenty-three people are trapped by quicksand in Morecambe Bay in England when the tide comes in, and they drown.

Don't Panic

What if you are alone when you fall into quicksand? The first important rule is to stay calm. You will sink if you struggle and thrash about with your arms and legs. It is a good idea to shed any extra weight you are carrying, such as a heavy backpack. Take off your shoes, too, especially if they are boots or heavy shoes. These could make it harder for you to get out.

July 2014

A 78-year-old Utah woman is trapped in quicksand in Arches National Park for 14 hours.

2005

Researchers at the University of Amsterdam publish their experiments with quicksand.

Once you are able to lie with your legs at the surface of quicksand, it is easier to swim or for someone to safely pull you out of it.

Find a Way to Float

Your body is lighter than the quicksand, so you can float in it on your back as you do in water. Start to lean back. Then wriggle your legs a little. This slightly agitates the soil, allowing water back in to soften it. Work slowly—moving fast sucks you in, but moving slowly allows you to gradually pull yourself out. When both legs reach the surface, you can crawl to solid land on your belly.

Sinking Experiments

People still have a lot to learn about quicksand. In the early 2000s, **physicist** Daniel Bonn and his team at the University of Amsterdam tested how far a person could really sink into quicksand. They did this with beads that were the same **density** as a human body, so they would float or sink as a person would. When dropped into quicksand, they floated on top. Even when shaken, the beads did not sink completely. The same would happen to a person.

Dry Quicksand

There have long been stories about another dangerous quicksand—dry quicksand. It is said to look exactly like the stable sand that surrounds it. Many people have doubted the tales about unsuspecting animals and humans being swallowed instantly by dry quicksand, sometimes during sandstorms. But in 2004, scientists in the Netherlands demonstrated that the tales could be true.

According to legend, the army of Persian ruler Cambyses II disappeared in a sandstorm in the 1st century BCE. Some people today attribute this loss to dry quicksand.

Traditional wet quicksand occurs when water flows into sand or soil, agitating it and becoming trapped. Physicist Detlef Lohse wondered what would happen

The film *Lawrence of Arabia* shows a character sinking into dry quicksand during a sandstorm.

if air instead of water agitated the soil. He and his team tried it with a container of sand.

They first forced air into the sand. When the sand settled, it looked exactly as it had before. Then they dropped a weighted Ping-Pong ball into it. The sand swallowed the ball immediately, sending a jet of sand into the air.

The team had demonstrated that the legends could be true. They also proved that dry quicksand could be even more dangerous than wet quicksand. It works much faster, objects sink deeper in it, and it is impossible to spot. Doubt remains, however, about how often dry quicksand might actually occur in nature.

Quick clay can cause
unexpected and
serious destruction.

Quicksand's Deadly Cousin

Quick clay is similar to quicksand. It is a combination of water and particles of earth. It can also liquefy under certain conditions. But that is where the resemblance ends. Quick clay can be far more destructive and deadly than quicksand, turning into sudden, unexpected, and uncontrollable clay slides.

Alaska has more quick clay than any other U.S. state.

Sudden Destruction

Quick clay is found mainly in regions that have large deposits of marine clay. As the **glaciers** of the last ice age shrank thousands of years ago, they left this clay behind. The clay is mixed with large amounts of water. Surface tension holds the clay together in a jellylike form. When disturbed, the clay can turn to a liquid ooze with frightening speed. The disturbance could be an earthquake. It could also be human activity, such as digging.

Unlike rockslides or avalanches, there is no warning before a quick clay slide.

Quick clay is often found in the areas surrounding Oslo, Norway.

Endangered Countries

Most marine clay deposits are found in northern countries. Among them are Norway, Sweden, Finland, Russia, and Canada. Some reach as far south as the United States. No country is more at risk of quick clay slides than Norway. Some of Norway's best farmland sits atop quick clay. As a result, large populations are located on this fertile land.

Some of the worst damage from the Rissa quick clay slide occurred in the village of Årnset.

Disaster in Norway

On April 29, 1978, in the Norwegian town of Rissa, a farmer dug out a section of his land. He planned to build a new wing on his barn. The digging caused a disturbance, however, setting off a huge clay slide. For five minutes, the land crumbled into a nearby lake. The farmer watched his entire farm float away at a speed of 20 miles (32 km) per hour.

One witness saw the clay slide coming toward him "like a sea wave." By the time it ended, it had swept away seven farms and five homes. Of the 40 people caught in the slide, only one died. People have not been so fortunate in other slides. A quick clay slide in 1893 in Verdal, Norway, killed 116 people. This was almost half of the village's population.

Deadly quick clay slides occur in the province of Quebec in Canada.

Testing and Prevention

In recent years, scientists have studied the land where marine clay can turn to quick clay. They have conducted tests to see how sensitive the clay is. In 1991, researchers analyzed the clay in Lemieux, Canada, near the city of Ottawa. Finding that the clay was potentially quite dangerous, they told the residents to abandon the town. It was good that everyone left. Two years later, a serious slide occurred there.

Glacial clay deposits cover many parts of Canada. Scientists test them to see how likely they are to turn into quick clay slides.

Understanding how quicksand works and how best to escape it can help make quicksand seem a little less scary.

Being Safe

Tests such as these help people prepare for possible quick clay slides. Scientists also continue to study traditional wet quicksand. They search for details about how quicksand works and where it is likely to be found. The information helps people know exactly how to recognize, avoid, and escape this dangerous substance, and remain safe. ★

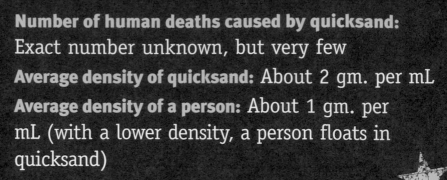

Number of human deaths caused by quicksand: Exact number unknown, but very few

Average density of quicksand: About 2 gm. per mL

Average density of a person: About 1 gm. per mL (with a lower density, a person floats in quicksand)

Continents known to have quicksand: All continents, except possibly Antarctica

States in the United States in which quicksand is common: Arizona, Colorado, Florida, Georgia, New Jersey, New Mexico, North Carolina, Utah, Washington

Habitats in which quicksand can be found: Marshes, swamps, streams, lakes, beaches, and some deserts

Did you find the truth?

Quicksand can be any kind of soil that is changed by a steady flow of water.

Most quicksand sucks people and animals down quickly, with little hope of escape.

Resources

Books

Campbell, Guy. *The Boys' Book of Survival: How to Survive Anything, Anywhere*. New York: Scholastic, 2009.

Roy, Ron. *The Quicksand Question*. New York: Random House, 2002.

Visit this Scholastic Web site for more information on quicksand:
★ www.factsfornow.scholastic.com
Enter the keyword **Quicksand**

Important Words

caravans (KAR-uh-vanz) — groups of people using animals or vehicles to travel together

debris (duh-BREE) — the pieces of something that has been broken or destroyed

density (DEN-si-tee) — a measure of how heavy or light an object is for its size

erodes (ih-ROHDZ) — wears away gradually by natural forces

fossils (FOSS-uhlz) — bones, shells, or other traces of an animal or plant from millions of years ago, preserved as rock

glaciers (GLAY-shurz) — slow-moving masses of ice formed from snow that falls and does not melt over many years

hypothermia (hye-poh-THUR-mee-uh) — a condition of having a dangerously low body temperature

liquefy (LIK-wuh-fye) — to make a solid into a liquid

mudflats (MUD-flats) — mud-covered stretches of land caused by tidal waters

physicist (FIZ-i-sist) — a person who studies matter and energy

predators (PRED-uh-turz) — animals that live by hunting other animals for food

saturate (SACH-uh-rate) — to soak thoroughly

Index

Page numbers in **bold** indicate illustrations.

About the Author

Steven Otfinoski has written more than 170 books for young readers. He has written books about blizzards, volcanoes, and other natural disasters. He also teaches writing at two universities in Connecticut, where he lives with his family.